Beyond Grief

Healing Life's Losses

William E. Rabior

Liguori
One Liguori Drive
Liguori MO 63057-9999

Imprimi Potest:
Thomas D. Picton, C.Ss.R.
Provincial, Denver Province
The Redemptorists

ISBN 0-7648-1353-6

Printed in the United States of America
09 08 07 06 05   5 4 3 2 1

Liguori Publications, a nonprofit corporation, is an apostolate of the Redemptorists. To learn more about the Redemptorists, visit *Redemptorists.com*.

To order, call 1-800-325-9521
www.liguori.org

Beyond Grief

Healing Life's Losses

William E. Rabior

Sally and Tim were happily married for twenty-seven years. One morning while shaving, Tim collapsed and died of a heart attack. He was only forty-nine.

It has been ten months since his funeral. Asked how she is doing, Sally replies: "The pain is still there. Sometimes it almost feels like there's a piece of barbed wire wrapped around my heart."

Kelli and David were married ten years. One day Kelli told him she didn't love him anymore and was filing for divorce. She added that there was another man in her life. David finds himself drinking more than he ever has, and sometimes he breaks into tears for no apparent reason. His feelings and actions often puzzle and confuse him.

Sam, fifty-seven, has been an accountant for a small company for the past thirty years. The company was recently bought out by a large corporation, and Sam has been informed that his services will no longer be needed.

"How can I possibly start over at my age?" he asks, panic in his voice. Lately, his blood pressure has been dangerously high. He sleeps only a few hours at night, then remains wide awake, worrying about his future.

Julia has just found out she has a rare eye disease that will soon destroy her sight. Her depression is so deep that her family fears she might become suicidal.

When her physician suggests sharing her feelings with someone might prove beneficial, she snaps back that she doesn't want to discuss anything with anyone, and her decision is final.

In each brief scenario, grieving is occurring. Whenever we lose someone or something significant, we are likely to grieve.

Grieving occurs not just when somebody close to us dies, but whenever there is any profound sense of loss. Divorce, the end of a friendship, the loss of a job, the loss of one's health, even a material loss such as the destruction of one's home may plunge us into grieving.

When this happens, each of us will grieve in our own way, at our own speed, influenced by our own unique personality, and from our past experiences of loss.

Grief is not an event, but a process that affects us physically, emotionally, and spiritually. For example, a grieving person may experience a variety of complaints, such as headaches, weight loss, insomnia, even physical pain. Emotionally, grief can give rise to anxiety, depression, and mood swings. Grieving may also affect our spiritual life, as Tina illustrates in the story below.

"When I had my third miscarriage in a row, I developed an irrational feeling God had either abandoned me or was punishing me. I became terrified about what he might do next. Eventually, my terror turned into rage toward him.

"Fortunately, talking with my pastor showed me my grieving had become impaired. He helped me work toward reestablishing a relationship with God. It took time."

She continued: "When I was alienated from God, the spiritual pain and loneliness were unbearable. For me, Grief Land was a dark place I never want to return to."

Understanding Grief

Although grief may give rise to the most intense pain we have ever experienced, it is not our enemy. It is, in fact, our ally that enables us to heal after a loss. Dr. Elisabeth Kubler-Ross, who pioneered research related to grieving, described the five stages or responses to grief as being denial, anger, bargaining, depression, and acceptance. She stressed that we may visit and revisit these responses over and over.

Other experts describe the grief process as having three components: the first is shock—the feeling this cannot be happening to me; the second, a feeling of disintegration—the world I have known is now falling apart; the third, reintegration—finding the strength to accept and live with the loss.

However it is described, grieving tends to be an arduous process that changes us forever. Often, there is no complete closure to our grieving following a significant loss. We may reexperience it again and again in varying forms and degrees of intensity for the rest of our lives.

Kinds of Grief

In addition, there are different kinds of grief. Delayed grief may surface weeks, months, or even years after a loss. Repressed emotions linked to an unresolved loss from the past may demand attention following a loss in the present. That is what happened to Alex.

"When my father died, I never shed a tear for him. I didn't want to appear weak in front of family and friends. I missed him deeply, but I wouldn't talk about my feelings with anyone. I just stuffed them all inside of me and ignored them. That approach worked for three years, until my son, my only child, graduated from high school and got ready to leave for college."

What happened then? Alex continued: "Something stirred inside of me. It was the grief for my dad I had tried to ignore. Now, it wanted my full attention."

He sighed. "I felt I just couldn't face another loss—not even something as normal as my son going off to school. My depression immobilized me. I couldn't even go to work. My doctor gave me antidepressant medication and sent me to a therapist, who helped me understand what was happening. I wish now I had done my grieving when dad died. It would have been easier on my family and me."

With anticipatory grief, a person goes through the phases of grieving prior to the loss. Then, when the actual loss takes place (for example, the death of a loved one who has long battled cancer), little grieving may occur, because most of the grief work has already been done.

Grief studies suggest women and men tend to grieve differently. Women often have better social-support systems, especially their close friends, which they can draw upon during the grieving process.

Men tend to keep their grief to themselves—bottling it up, suppressing, or denying it. They may lose themselves in a flurry of activity or escape into their work to avoid having to grieve. As a result, they are vulnerable to serious depression. Jim and Phyllis talked about what happened to them.

"Our youngest son, Jason, was killed by a car while riding his bike," Phyllis said. "For a time I wanted to die, too, but I kept talking out my feelings with my closest friends and crying until I couldn't cry anymore. After a while I started to act like my old self, but I really worried about Jim."

Jim nodded: "With good reason. I left planet Earth for a while. I withdrew. I wouldn't talk to anyone, not even her. Instead, I went fishing. I would drive to the fishing spots where Jason and I had fished. I'd get out my gear, but wouldn't bait the hook. I'd just throw the line into the water, so it looked like I was fishing. Then, I'd sit on the riverbank and sob my heart out.

"Phyllis healed a lot faster than I did. My grieving was very private. I allowed no one to help me. I wouldn't recommend my style of grieving to anyone. It took too long to come out of the darkness. Besides, it's just too painful to grieve all by yourself. Grief, like happiness, is meant to be shared with somebody else."

Grief Work

The aim of grief work is not to erase the memories of what we have experienced so we become amnesiacs, but to make those memories less painfully controlling. Grief work is seldom a once-and-for-all event. It tends to be repetitive. Usually, we need to express our grief over and over, until we come to a place of peace and acceptance.

Grieving is the hardest work any of us will ever do. It can be so difficult and demanding that the temptation is to ignore it, hoping it will go away. It may or may not.

Ignoring our grief may prove to be dangerous to our well-being. Unresolved grief can take a toll on our peace of mind. It can affect us in ways we may not even recognize. That is what happened to Stan.

"I was only two years from retirement, when I put most of our life's savings into the stock market. There was a big downturn, and I was annihilated. My wife forgave me and told me to let it go, but I couldn't. At first, I was mostly angry at myself, but soon I became angry at the whole world.

"In fact, I became so hostile, finally my wife couldn't take it anymore. She insisted I get professional help, and eventually I did. Counseling showed me that I was grieving the loss of our financial resources, and my anger came from feelings of humiliation and my unwillingness to forgive myself and letting my family down.

"I still wince whenever I hear a stock market report, but now I am only angry occasionally. Grieving can make you bitter or better. In my case it was both."

Coping Suggestions

The single best way to process grief is to talk it out with someone we trust. That person may be a friend, a clergy person, or a professional counselor. Look in the Yellow Pages of your telephone directory under "Grief Counseling Services" for the names of counselors who specialize in grief issues.

Many churches and communities have support groups for the grieving. Check the public-service ads in your local newspaper. Remember that asking for help is a sign of courage, not weakness. It means you want a better life for yourself.

Writing down feelings has also helped many grieving persons find solace. After the death of a loved one, for example, some even write letters to the deceased as a means of coping. Others find that keeping a journal of their thoughts and feelings provides valuable insights into their grieving experiences.

Exercise is also recommended by grief professionals. Walking is an effective way to fight the depression arising from grieving. But inactivity, for example, becoming a couch potato, only makes us feel worse.

If you are grieving, be extra kind to yourself. Be your own best friend. Pamper yourself. If you have an opportunity to do something pleasurable or something that brings you comfort, make time for it.

Finally, the Scriptures repeatedly tell us God is always there for us when we hurt. God suffers with those who suffer. He understands our pain. Letting go and letting God help us handle our loss can free us from our agitation and deep unhappiness. Prayer in particular can heal even the deepest grief.

And that is why the second part of this pamphlet contains various prayers written to help persons struggling with the pain of loss. You are welcome to use these prayers, but I also encourage you to talk directly to God in your own words—words that flow from a wounded heart and spirit. God will hear you.

I have written these prayers with the hope they will help hurting hearts heal, and that those who pray them will come to experience solace and peace in their life, along with new hope and even happiness once again.

Prayers for Times of Loss

When Your Spouse Dies

Lord Jesus, since ______ died, I am not the same. It's as though part of me died with her (him). It feels like wintertime in my soul, and my heart is so filled with pain I think it's going to break in two. There's also a jumble of mixed emotions swirling inside of me. Some days I actually feel like dying myself, so I can be with her (him). I even find myself getting furious at ______ for dying and leaving me. And then there's the numbing loneliness—a single place at the dinner table, only one menu in a restaurant, the emptiness on her (his) side of the bed.

I find myself wanting, wishing, that ______ was back with me, yet I know that would be unfair to her (him). Now that she (he) had stepped into eternity to be with you, her (his) destiny has been fulfilled. I can't take that away. The Scriptures say love is as strong as death, but I believe in an even greater truth. Love can actually be stronger than death. Your life and love proved that. Death ends a life, but not a relationship. My love for ______ will go on as long as I live. Carry that love to ______ right now, and may it touch her (him) even in eternity.

Thank you for the life we shared together, for the time we had, and for the great gift ______ was to me. I commend her (him) to your love and mercy. In the meantime, Lord, help me in every way, every day. Help me rebuild my life without

______. Bless me with strength, guidance, and the will to go on. May ______ rest in your peace, Lord Jesus, and may that same peace heal and console me. Amen.

When a Family Member Dies

Dear Lord, I still have a hard time believing ______ is gone. When I think about his (her) death, I feel numb. Sometimes, it all seems like a bad dream from which I will awaken and ______ will be with me again. Grief is such a hard thing to shake, Lord. It's like a nagging toothache—a dull throbbing pain in my heart that won't let up no matter what I do.

I don't want to let go of ______, yet I know I must. But because of my faith in you, I believe I am not really letting go forever. Life has been changed for ______, but not ended. There's an old saying that where there's life, there's hope. But because of you, Lord Jesus, even where there is death, there is hope. I believe

______ is with you now, and one day I will be with you, too, and see him (her) again. I cling to that hope with all my heart.

Meanwhile, I don't want to just keep the memory of ______ alive. I want to keep his (her) finest qualities alive in and through me. What I loved most about ______ I want to incorporate into my own life, so that others can still encounter him (her) in me. That will be my ongoing gift to ______.

Thank you for all that we shared together, and for the many ways I was gifted by him (her). May the joy, peace, and love of your kingdom be his (hers) to overflowing, and through this prayer send him (her) my love as well. Amen.

When a Friend Dies

Lord Jesus, the Scriptures say a faithful friend is a sturdy shelter, and in finding one we find a treasure. With the death of______, I feel as though my treasure has been stolen.

I feel impoverished and lost. Lord, you know how much ______ meant to me. The world seems so empty and cold now without her (him). I never knew I could miss anyone so much.

Lord Jesus, you know what I'm talking about. You understand my grieving, because you once lost a dear friend, too. When Lazarus died, you cried for him the way I have cried for ______. Then, you proclaimed a message of hope our world has never heard before or since. You said you are the resurrection and the life, and whoever believes in you will not die forever. Help me to cling to that great promise of hope, Lord. Because of you, I believe I will see ______ in the land of the living and know her (his) friendship once again. Through my faith in your promises may I come to peace of mind and heart.

Until we meet again, I commend ______ to your great love. Amen.

When a Relationship Ends

Dear God, I love ______ so much, but now he (she) has chosen a life without me, and the hurt and emptiness are overwhelming. I know that friends are not possessions, and people have the right to make choices about relationships. So, as much as I am able at the present moment, I forgive and release ______. In forgiving and letting go, may I experience peace. Bless ______ in every possible way and take care of him (her). I pray for only the best in his (her) life. Now, may I find the strength to reach out to others and build new relationships. Amen.

After Some Significant Loss

Loving God, no one close to me has died, and things could be much worse in my life, yet I've lost ______, and this loss upsets me. What I had was very important to me, and now that it's gone, I realize I'm grieving for it. God, help me to keep things in perspective. The most important thing in life is my relationship with you. All else pales in comparison—something I need to remember always.

At the same time, I believe that as your son (daughter) I can bring this matter to you and pray with an expectant faith that you will not only help me deal with this loss, but even more, that you will make all things work together for good in my life, because I belong to you and love you. For all your good gifts, graces, and blessings of the past, present, and future, I thank you and praise you, gracious God. Amen.

For Others Who Are Grieving

Compassionate God, because of my own personal loss, I am grieving now, but I am also aware that others around me are grieving, too. My loss may seem great, but theirs may well be greater. At this moment we are all united in a common bond of grief, so even as I pray for myself, I pray for them, too. Be their Good Shepherd, Good God, as well as mine. Walk with us through this dark valley to new light and hope. Console us with your tender mercies and your healing grace. Amen.

For Growth From Grief

Lord Jesus, I pray that this grief I am experiencing will not be without value for me, for others, and for you. Let me grow from my grieving. Let me become a better person, more caring and compassionate, so this grieving of mine will not have been in vain.

May my grief make me more sensitive and responsive to the hurts and needs of others. May I never forget the importance of a kind word, a loving touch, or a patient smile offered to those in pain. I know how valuable the ministry of presence is. Let me recognize those times when I need not say or do a thing to help another hurting human being except be present to listen and to love.

Help me grow from my grief, Lord. May it become a tool in your hands, to shape and transform me into someone more like you. Someday, I may even be able to thank you for the experience of this grief, because of the good fruit brought forth from it by your gift of grace.

For what you have done, are doing, and are yet to do in and through me, I thank and praise you, Lord Jesus. Amen.